Helping Children See Jesus

ISBN: 978-1-64104-105-8

Forever Changed By The Book
The Jo Shetler Story

Authors: Edie Cunningham, Karen Weitzel, with Joanne Shetler
Illustrator: Eric Minoura
Graphic Artists: Ian Brownlie, Yuko Kishimoto
Page Layout: Patricia Pope

© 2020 Bible Visuals International
PO Box 153, Akron, PA 17501-0153
Phone: (717) 859-1131
www.biblevisuals.org

RELATED ITEMS

To access related items (such as activities, memory verse posters and translated texts) please visit our web store at shop.biblevisuals.org and enter 5135 in the search box on the page.

FREE TEXT DOWNLOAD

To access a FREE printable copy of the teaching text (PDF format) in English or other available languages, enter S5135DL in the search box. Add the item to your cart, and use coupon code XTACSV17 at checkout. Once your order is processed you will receive an email with a link to the free download.

STUDENT ACTIVITES

These are included with the FREE printable copy of the English teaching text for this story. See the directions under Free Text Download (above) to access them.

"Hi, I'm Doming, a Balangao boy from Botac. Meet my gentle "Carabao," or water buffalo! When the tropical sun is unbearable she lays in a wet mud hole to cool off. Her weight? Just 1,300 pounds! Do you like her drooped neck and wide horns which curl at the ends? She'd never win a race, but she can pull a heavy wagonload of rice to market."

"My dad cut down a tree and carved out a game we call SUNKA. We use shells for game pieces." (See rules on page 24.)

The flag of the Republic of the Philippines

"We Balangao are proud of our beautiful red, blue and white handwoven cloth. Do you like my wraparound skirt?"

• Botac
• Bagabag

Manila •

"I make beautiful music with my nose flute! You can't blow with your lips!"

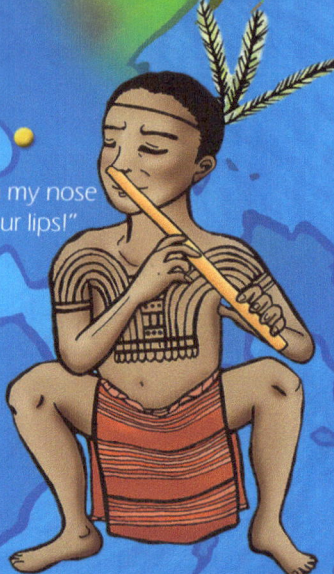

"Hi, my name is Loree. I eat cooked corn on a stick! Look ma, no messy fingers! And a real treat is roasted beetles! They crunch like potato chips!"

"Rice planting is backbreaking work. While the rice grows, the terrace gardens look like huge green steps. When the rice kernels are ripe, the rice stalk is cut off. We club the stalks in a deep hollowed-out log. The outside rice 'germ' falls off and we get hard white rice to cook in big aluminum pots. We grow enough rice here to feed ourselves. We eat it every day–piles of it!"

"The Bird of Paradise won't fly! It is one of the exotic, colorful flowers that grows here. But it does look like a bird!"

"Sweep up the dirt with a tiger grass broom, and then clean the mud off the floors. No problem! I just cut a coconut in half, expose the rough fibers in between the outside shell and inside coconut meat. This makes a great brush to hop onto and 'swish' back and forth with my foot!"

"As many as 20 people fit inside and hang off the back of our colorfully decorated taxi called a Jeepney*. People, baggage and even chickens ride on the top!"

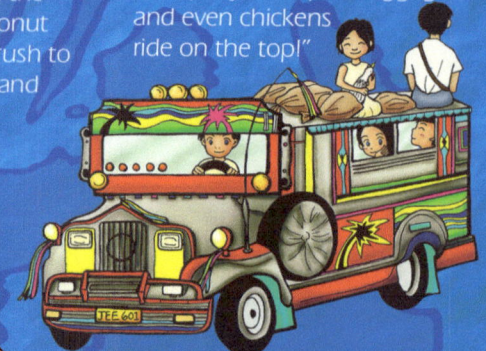

"Every night I roll out my mat made of soft woven leaves to sleep on. It's my bed!"

*Exclusive to the Philippines but not found in Botac

"Our pigs, rooster and chickens live under our house-on-stilts."

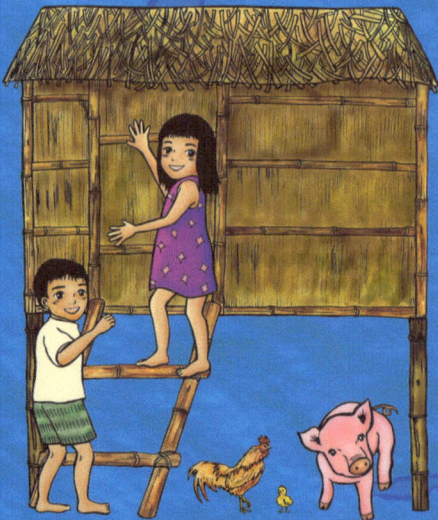

A great multitude, which no man could number, of all nations, and kindreds, and peoples, and tongues, stood before the throne, and before the Lamb . . . and cried with a loud voice, saying, "Salvation to our God."

Revelation 7:9, 10

The truck engine roared to a start when seven-year-old Joanne turned the key in the ignition. She sputtered, *Now what? I don't know how to drive this truck!* Joanne, Jo as her friends called her, panicked. *What were Dad's blunt instructions? "Get the truck,"* he'd said. *"Drive it to me in the field."* When she protested that she didn't know how, he'd told her, *"I didn't ask if you knew how. I just told you to do it!"*

Show Illustration #1

Once the motor was humming, Jo fiddled with her foot until she found the clutch and pushed down on it. Then she yanked the stick shift from neutral straight into second gear and eased up on the clutch. The pickup lurched ahead like a bucking bronco. Jo worked the unfamiliar pedals until the truck steadied and moved forward.

She stared through the windshield in fear and amazement. "How'd I do that?" she gasped. "Oh, who cares! The truck's going!" She aimed the truck for the open fence gate and got through it. Her dad waited in the massive field near a high mound of garden weeds they'd uprooted earlier.

"The brake! Where's the brake? I've got to stop this thing!" she cried, wide-eyed with fear. Finding the brake, Jo shoved it down with both feet and all her weight.

Jo's dad jumped out of the way as the truck careened toward him and abruptly stalled. He wasn't happy. Jo wasn't catching on to driving like his two sons had when they were young. Though it was a rough ride, Jo had done it exactly as her dad had required.

Trembling, she didn't look at her dad as she slid out of the cab. Without a word between them, they silently piled the weeds high on the truck bed.

Joanne lived with her parents and brothers, Wayne and Art, on their thousand-acre farm in central California. There were so many fields, valleys, fruit orchards, and woods that one could barely see the rooftops of the closest neighbors.

One Friday afternoon several years later when Jo was eleven, she and her brothers were riding home on the school bus. As they bolted down the bus steps, the driver, Pastor Brown, called after them, "Hey, kids, we're having some special children's meetings all next week at church after school. Ask your folks if you can attend them. You'd love the Gospel magician! I'll bring you back home each day if they say it's okay."

"Okay," said Wayne as the Shetler kids waved and ran towards their farmhouse. The kids were hesitant to ask for time off from afternoon farm chores to attend the kids' meetings for five afternoons straight. But they would ask anyway.

Wayne, Art and Jo filed in as the porch screen closed with a bang. Mrs. Shetler, home from her shift as head nurse at the local hospital, greeted the children as they dropped their schoolbooks and lunch boxes on the kitchen counter. The boys quickly changed into work clothes, ate a snack and headed outdoors to do their jobs. Jo went after the cows to herd them in for the five o'clock milking.

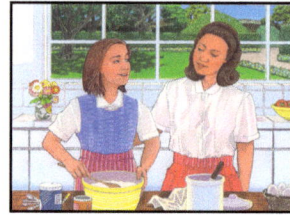

Show Illustration #2

Then, back in the kitchen, Jo grabbed her apron and tied it behind her. "I love working in the kitchen with you, Mom."

"Are you glad it's Friday?" Jo's mom inquired.

"Yeah," Jo said. "You know that I like school, but by Friday I feel like one of those cooped-up chickens out in the hen house."

Mrs. Shetler laughed. "Mix up a batch of biscuits," she instructed, "and then go take care of those cooped-up chickens. Laddie is waiting outside for you. He'd love a good run."

"Okay." Soon a cloud of white flour swirled in the air around Jo's face. "Mom, as a nurse, what's it like to give a shot to a patient? Did you ever see a person die? Maybe I'll grow up and be a nurse–a good one–just like you, Mom."

Mrs. Shetler gave Jo a loving look. "I think you'd make a great nurse, Joanne." Giving her daughter a gentle whack, she added, "Now, get busy. You've got to take care of those animals before dinner."

Jo dashed from the house and headed for the barn. She whistled for Laddie. The collie dog shook himself from sleep and bounded towards Jo. They ran side by side to the chicken house. Jo finished her chores and returned to help her mom fix dinner. Then she called the family in to eat.

Show Illustration #3

When the Shetler family was seated around the dinner table, Art and Wayne dug into the beef stew and biscuits. It appeared as if they'd not eaten all day.

"Slow down a bit, Wayne, or you won't be getting any birthday cake," their dad warned.

The kids never talked back to their parents. But Wayne got up his nerve and blurted out, "Dad, Joanne already stole my candy bar earlier today. Please, I want a piece of my birthday cake!"

Jo's brothers glared at her. Her face turned bright red with embarrassment. Not wanting to look at her parents, Jo dropped her head and stared down at her plate.

Art spoke u"What do you call that kind of candy bar, Joanne? A *paper* Milky Way® candy bar?"

Mr. and Mrs. Shetler exchanged glances. Jo's dad demanded, "Do you have something to tell us, Joanne?"

[Delay…] "But I was just trying to play a joke," Jo said sheepishly. "After all, Wayne's birthday is on April Fool's Day!" Then Jo's tone changed, "I was only getting even for all the times he's bullied me."

"Please, Joanne," Mrs. Shetler stopped Jo. "We'll talk about that later. Wayne's birthday cake will be on the table soon."

Show Illustration #4

Later, as promised, Mom entered Jo's bedroom and sat on the edge of the bed. Sprawled across the bed, Jo sat up with a jerk. She defiantly crossed her arms against her chest and blurted out, "I don't know why I ate Wayne's candy bar."

"Joanne," Mother explained, "it was a big deal to Wayne because that candy bar was one of his few birthday gifts. You know we can't afford a lot of extras right now."

"Yeah," Jo said reluctantly. Then she confessed, "After I ate the candy bar, I stuffed the empty wrapper with paper and resealed it! It looked unopened."

"Well, it was a joke to you, but it wasn't a joke to Wayne. You made him very angry," Jo's mom said, gently laying her hand on Jo's shoulder.

"Do you know why I did it, Mom? It was my way of getting back at Wayne. Sometimes when you're not looking, he's a big bully. He even beats up on me. And Art always leaves half his work for Wayne and me to finish. And then I have to make lunches every day for my brothers." Jo could barely catch her breath as she worked her way down through her "what's-wrong-with-the-world list." Then she added, "And Dad never compliments me. He thinks I'll get a swelled head or something. Oh, who cares anyway?" Jo burst into tears.

"Your Dad and I care, Joanne." With those loving words, Joanne hugged her mom and apologized between sobs.

"In the morning," Mrs. Shetler said, "we'll be waiting for you to tell Wayne you're sorry. And Joanne, I'll talk to your dad about the other things you've said. Good night now, dear." Comforted, Jo soon fell asleep.

The next morning, somehow before Saturday morning chores, Jo managed to squeak out an apology to Wayne.

Monday came and it was back to school. Having cleared it with their parents, the Shetler kids went to the children's meetings at Pastor Brown's church. Kids had come from miles around and the church was packed. Jo found that she liked the special program. She sang songs with the others about God's love and how kids could believe what the Bible said was true.

Show Illustration #5

A tall gentleman, the Gospel magician, stepped in front of the children. Excitement was in the air.

Jo poked Art and whispered, "Why do you think the magician is wearing that funny tall black hat?"

The stovepipe hat sat squarely on the magician's head. Then he removed it and tipped it towards the kids and asked, "What's in this hat?" All the kids leaned forward to look inside. He stuck his hand into the hat.

In unison the kids called out, "It's empty!"

Then the magician pulled his hand out of the hat and . . . poof, like magic, a beautiful golden scarf suddenly appeared. The children stared in amazement. One child shouted, "Where'd you get the scarf? That hat was empty!"

The magician talked kindly as he waved the golden scarf in midair over the children's heads. "This gold scarf reminds me of Heaven, that beautiful city where God is. The streets there are made of gold. There is no nighttime, no sadness, no anger, no sickness, and no one ever dies in Heaven because God is there. God loves you very much and wants you to go to live with Him in Heaven someday when you are done living on earth."

Sounds like a very special place, Jo thought. She'd often wondered about Heaven. She liked that part about there being no anger in Heaven because there seemed to be plenty to go around on earth. But she'd never talked to God before. It was surprising to hear that God loved her. *I don't even know God, so how could He love me?* Jo wondered as she continued listening.

Mysteriously, the magician pulled yet another scarf from his "empty" hat. "Do you see this dark scarf?" he asked.

In unison the kids yelled, "Yes!"

"The darkness of this scarf makes me think of sin," the magician said. (*Teacher*: See John 3:19.) "Have you ever done wrong things when your parents weren't around just like I did at your age?"

Jo quickly thought of the wrong things her brothers did, things that always seemed so mean to her. (*Teacher*: Explain that it's always easier to see someone else's wrongs rather than your own.)

The magician continued, "But if you think you've never broken any of God's laws, the Bible says we *all* have. We were born with sin in us–a "wanting to do wrong things." Then the magician opened his Bible and actually proved what he'd said. (*Teacher*: Read aloud Romans 3:23.)

"The wrong things you do prove you're separated from God Who loves you. Your sin will make you miss living in God's Heaven, and this is a huge problem! There can be no sin in Heaven. God says sin must be punished."

Jo squirmed. This was serious!

The magician pulled a third scarf from his hat. "This red scarf tells us of some *wonderful* news! We have an escape from the punishment for sin! God did something special. He sent His Son, the Lord Jesus, to die on the cross in our place so we won't have to take the punishment for our sin! Jesus gave His life and shed His blood so that He could forgive our sins. He could do that because He didn't have any sin. Jesus took the punishment that we deserve. God put all of our sin on Jesus when He died on the cross."

This sounded like the best news Jo had ever heard!

Then, again out of nowhere, the magician pulled a beautifully clean, white scarf from his hat. "God is willing to forgive every sin you've done and make your heart, the real 'you,' even cleaner than this white scarf. God can do this for you because after Jesus died on the cross and was buried, God raised Him back to life on the third day! God accepted Jesus' dying for the sin of everyone. Jesus is alive now, He's waiting in Heaven, and He wants to come to you, forgive your sin and live in you." (*Teacher*: Read aloud Romans 10:9.)

Then, flash, another scarf was pulled out of the hat. "What color is this?" the magician asked.

"Green!" the children shouted.

"If you invite Jesus to be your Saviour, He comes to live in you and helps you grow to know God better. Grass grows, green things grow, and you can grow too. Every time you read Bible verses, talk to God, or hear the pastor teach from the Bible in church, if you obey, you will grow to be stronger and stronger followers of Jesus."

Though the room was crowded with kids, Jo felt as if she were the only person there. She felt as if the teacher were speaking directly to her though, of course, he was talking to all the kids.

Glad that no one could hear her thoughts, Jo struggled with all the things she'd heard. *God loves me and wants to forgive me? He wants me to have eternal life? This is the best news I've ever heard! I want that!* So when the teacher asked if any of the kids wanted to know Jesus as their Saviour, Jo shot her hand up into the air.

She slipped out of her seat to talk to Pastor Brown who showed her verses from the Bible. As sincerely as she knew how, Jo prayed, "Dear God, thank You for loving me even though You know I've done lots of wrong things. I'm so sorry for my sins. I believe that Jesus died for my sins. Please forgive me and come live in me. Amen." Suddenly a new joy flooded Jo's heart.

Jo had just prayed the most important prayer of her life! She'd prayed to become part of God's family, something she'd never done before or ever dreamed about doing. This was much more important than even her dream of having a beautiful house on a hill with a white picket fence.

(*Teacher:* Ask children if they would like to know Jesus as their Saviour. Invite them to talk to you or other teachers about this most important decision. Designate an area in your classroom where children may meet with you to receive counseling.)

Chapter 2
A Step at a Time

Show Illustration #6

One Sunday at church when Jo was 13, a missionary spoke. Jo enjoyed hearing missionary adventures. But something this man said shocked her: "Ninety percent of those who are sharing the Gospel are doing it among just 10 percent of the world's population. That leaves only 10 percent of the "go-ers", "tell-ers" and makers of disciples to reach the other 90 percent of the world's people."

The words hit Jo hard! *Oh no,* she thought. *That's not what I wanted to hear. Now I'll have to be a missionary–whatever they are.* How would she ever get out of going? God's Word commanded it, and the need was so great. Becoming a missionary was the only choice Jo could make, even if it wasn't what she really wanted to do.

On the next Sunday night another missionary challenged the young people by saying, "If God is calling you to be a missionary, you should start praying right now for the people you'll go to some day." And from that day on, Jo did. She prayed almost every day for those people to whom God would one day send her to tell the good news of Jesus, whoever they were and wherever they lived.

Now Jo's ears were really up like antennas whenever missionaries spoke. "It can get lonely when you're far from relatives and you face many dangers," some missionaries shared. "And sometimes it's very discouraging, especially when you've told people the Gospel over and over, but they still resist obeying the Lord Jesus." And missionaries almost always had a story about eating some horrible food.

Then one night at church, a movie about Africa was shown. Jo was captivated by the African children who had become Christians. They were laughing and so happy. Suddenly being a missionary was starting to excite Jo. She prayed, *Lord, if that's what the Gospel does to people, I want to be a missionary and see those kinds of results–people really happy because they've come to know Jesus.*

But other times Jo was troubled by unanswered questions: *What exactly does a missionary do? How do they know when they've finished their work? I want to do something that will last forever. Will anything I do really last? F-o-r-e-v-e-r?*

Jo had lots of questions, but there was one thing she did know about being a missionary: she would need to learn another language. *That* seemed impossible; Jo didn't like languages.

Three years later sixteen-year-old Jo quietly approached her mom and asked, "Mom, it's Tuesday night. So, do you think Dad would let me drive the car to town?"

"Probably," Mom said as she laid another shirt on the ironing board. "You're a good driver. Why don't you ask him?"

Show Illustration #7

Since Mr. Shetler was reading the evening paper, Jo spoke quietly, "It's Tuesday night, Dad. Do you suppose I could take the car to Pastor Brown's Bible study? I've finished cleaning up the supper dishes; I've got my homework done; I've . . ."

Her dad's words cut in mid-sentence, "You may take the car."

"Thank you, Dad!" Jo called as she lifted the keys off their hook and dashed to the family car.

Jo rambled down the long, winding country roads toward town. She talked to God as she drove. *I'm so excited to be part of the high school church grouI can talk to Pastor Brown about anything. He really listens to me and answers all my questions. And we get to study any part of the Bible we want. I'm glad the group is small 'cause big groups scare me. I wish I weren't so shy in big groups. Lord, when I finish high school, what's next? I want to do something with my life that will last forever. But what? The Bible will guide me, but I'm just not sure how to know.*

Show Illustration #8

At the Browns' home, all the teen-agers who were sitting around the living room had Bibles on their laps. Jo fingered the pages of her own Bible, thinking to herself, *I've got so much to learn about this Book.* The Tuesday night Bible study had become one of Jo's favorite weekly events.

From that night on Jo never missed the Bible study. Jo learned more about the Bible and how God wants all of one's life. Jo began to grow concerned. *Sometimes I think this is more than I bargained for! This is going to demand my whole life. I've always wanted to live in a big house on a hill with a white picket fence around it and have lots of animals in the barn. I thought being a Christian was something one just did as they planned out their own life.*

Pastor Brown was never shocked by Jo's honest comments, even the time she'd told him, "I think I might just quit being a Christian–it's too hard." Pastor Brown knew that God was working in Jo's life, and he wisely let her work through her questions and concerns.

Jo longed to share about God with others, but her high school classmates weren't interested. Younger kids were different. They listened, they could think, they responded, and they could make good decisions about life. Pastor Brown knew how Jo felt. One Sunday morning after church he stopped her and said, "I know you'd really like to teach the Bible to children. There's a way you can learn how. We have a class that meets here on Wednesdays after school. The teacher tells the story to you in the very way you tell it to the kids." Jo was excited!

Every Wednesday she listened to the instructors who knew how to work with kids. *They know what makes kids tick,* Jo thought, *and they have pictures we can use, too.* This was wonderful! Every Friday after school Jo walked to a house in town where 12 to 20 neighborhood kids gathered for a Good News Club®. She taught the Bible lessons, and another lady taught the Gospel songs. Jo thanked God over and over as she helped many of the kids receive Jesus as Saviour.

After high school, Jo went to Bible college. After graduating, she took a one-year course in missionary medicine which she loved. Then she signed up for a summer course about languages so she could go into any country, learn their language, and be able to tell them about the Lord Jesus.

While studying at the summer linguistics school, Jo also learned about Bible translation. This school taught people how to learn an unwritten language, how to create an alphabet for that language and how to teach people to read and write. People who wanted to be Bible translators needed this language training in order to make the Bible available to people who have never had it in their language. Jo thought: *Bible translation would be one way to evangelize at least part of the world. I would know my job was finished when I translated to the end of the book!* The summer days passed. One day Jo remembered, *I always wanted to do something that would last forever. There are only two things that last forever: people and the Word of God. Giving people the Bible will have a "forever" effect on their lives.*

At the end of summer it really hit Jo: *If I give people God's Word in their own language, God Himself will speak to them just as He speaks to me. I won't have to worry about not telling them exactly all they need to know. The Bible will!* That was it! Jo had never been so excited. God wanted her to be a Bible translator!

Jo sat spellbound when a Bible translator from South America spoke. "The people where I live and work have never had their language written. They didn't have an alphabet. They had never seen a book, and they didn't even know how to write their names."

Adults who can't read? Jo hadn't thought about that before. *We learn to read and write in the first grade.*

The missionary continued, "These people have never had even one copy of God's Word in their language. When I dedicated my life to God He gave me the privilege of living among these people to learn their language and customs. We estimate it will take 15 to 20 years of working with them to translate God's Word into their heart language."

"Heart language," Jo learned, is the language a person dreams in, jokes in, and speaks with no effort. *English would be my heart language,* Jo reasoned.

The missionary then asked the students in the chapel program, "How many Bibles do you have in your home? As you call out the numbers, I'll tally the count."

That's easy to calculate, Jo said to herself. *Mom and Dad have one; Art, Wayne and I each have one. There are four Bibles in our house!*

(*Teacher:* Ask your students to count the number of Bibles they and/or their family own.)

After all the students answered, the missionary announced the final count. "That's over 300 Bibles just among us! We have been blessed to have so many Bibles in English. Let's pray for the thousands of people around the world who still don't have even ONE copy of God's Word in their language."

Jo couldn't stop thanking God for what He was leading her to do. She joined a group called Wycliffe Bible Translators to become a Bible translator.

Jo's next step was to go to Wycliffe's jungle training, a survival school in Mexico. *This is going to be fun,* she thought as she ordered what was on the list of needed equipment. *I'll need a duffle bag, a water canteen, some water purifying tablets, a waterproof container for matches, a waterproof flashlight, a plastic tarp–guess we'll be in some rain. I'll need a sleeping bag, insect repellent, malaria medicine, and a jungle hammock. This is going to be a great adventure.* When her equipment arrived, Jo was so excited she strung up her hammock between the clothesline poles to try it out!

Jo was teamed up with Anne in the jungle-training program. She'd met Anne at the summer linguistics course. The two women worked well together in the jungle. They were *champa* mates, assigned to work together to build their *champa,* a jungle shelter. The poles and main frame were made of wood from cutting down little trees in the rain forest, and they gathered special leaves for a roof. Together they built a mud stove where they would cook for the next six weeks. Down a secluded trail they built their own outhouse, a hole in the ground with very little around it except jungle! And they learned how to fight off bugs and other pesky critters.

Jo enjoyed Anne and was glad they had been assigned to work together. Anne was friendly, adventuresome, and didn't seem to be afraid of anything. When the guys swamped a huge canoe far up river, Anne was one of the gang that went out to help them recover it. With Anne leading the way, Jo was less shy and became more confident.

Wycliffe sends single women out as teams, two by two. About a year later Jo and Anne decided to team up to do Bible translation for a people grouAnne had asked to be assigned to the country of greatest need at the time. So, months later Jo and Anne were in the Philippines. Hiking through the mountains of the northern island of Luzon (lew-zon') was the only way to reach the Balangao (Bah-lahng'-ow) people, a tribe of headhunters who did not have the Bible in their language.

Show Illustration #9

As Jo and Anne hiked the steep mountains in the rain on their way to the Balangao region, Jo moaned, "I'm exhausted and my muscles ache. And look at our clothes! They'll never be clean again!" The two missionaries were led by another Wycliffe translator, Lawrence Reid (Laurie to his friends). Along with a group of people hired to carry their supplies, they hiked up and down steep mountains all day in constant rain and through slippery mud.

Jo sighed. Taking the ship from California to Manila (Mah-nil'-lah), the capital city of the Philippines, had been easy compared to this. And then there were those three days riding old buses around dangerous, curvy mountainous roads that took them far away from all the conveniences of modern life in Manila. Now this rough two-day hike was the last leg of the journey. It would take them into the Balangao territory where Jo and Anne hoped to live in one of the many villages.

Jo and Anne sloshed on, mud spattering their skirts and covering their sneakers. As they paused to rest on the steep trail, Jo thought, *And to think I thought the Philippines was a flat, hot, isolated sand bar in the Pacific with just coconut trees. But look at these mountains, these huge trees, and all the beautiful orchids hanging down.*

Anne bent down and removed *another* leech from her legs. "These bloodsuckers will be the death of me!"

"How many does that make?" Jo asked, checking her own legs.

"Too many!" said an exhausted Anne. "How many more mountains do you think we'll need to hike over until we get there? It's a good thing people at home are praying for us."

Laurie, the seasoned Wycliffe translator, smiled and called out, "The reason this is so steep is because we're taking the Balangao shortcut straight up!" Jo and Anne glanced up and saw how the trail veered straight upwards to the top of Mount Aggugu (Ag-koo-koo). The top was barely visible through the jungle growth.

The unbelievably steep climb finally ended in a clearing. Everyone paused to look at the beauty spread before them in the not-too-distant valley. Jo and Anne gasped at the wonder of it all. As far as they could see, mountains ringed a valley full of rice terraces that stair-stepped up the sides of the mountains. "It's one of the most beautiful sights I've ever seen!" Jo exclaimed. "I've heard that these Philippine rice terraces are called the eighth wonder of the world."

"Yes," Anne agreed, "and it'll be the ninth wonder of the world if we ever get there. We still have another full day of hiking ahead of us."

"Once we get there, we'll never leave!" Jo said. "We won't be able to make it back over these mountains."

After a rest the trek continued. Part of the time they walked on the rice terrace walls. Jo was worried. "Look at this, Anne. This path on the edge of the terrace can't be more than six inches wide. Be careful. These muddy rocks are so slippery!"

Laurie pointed to the brim of the rice terrace and cautioned the women, "If you slip, be sure you fall on the 'up' side. You'll only be in above your knees in mud and water. But if you fall on the 'down' side, it could be a 15-foot drop into the terrace below!"

Cautiously Jo and Anne inched their way along the top of the high rock walls that formed the terraces. Laurie chatted as he walked nimbly along the narrow path, "These terraces will be a beautiful emerald green when the rice grows." Jo and Anne kept their eyes glued to the path and the next step in front of them. Looking at the beauty around them would have to wait until later.

At the end of each terrace's trail, large stones stuck out from the wall forming stairs down (or up) to the next terrace. At the end of the rainy day, they finally arrived at Kadaklan (Kah-dahk-lahn), a village of one-room thatched houses, each on four-foot-high stilts. Black, bristly-haired pigs grunted beneath the raised houses. Clucking chickens pecked the ground looking for rice that might have fallen through the bamboo floor above.

"Welcome to Kadaklan! We're halfway to Balangao!" Laurie announced.

Show Illustration #10

In Kadaklan Jo and Anne saw an old woman sitting on her haunches before a spring of water, her knees nearly touching her chin. A hollow bamboo pipe stuck out from the hill and clear water gushed onto the ground. This was the village water supply. The woman was washing her enamel plates and cups.

Jo noticed some wood houses, especially one house that had walls of some kind of woven reeds. A boy had just arrived there with a full basket of rice bundles. He stood beside a two-foot-high upright log that had been hollowed out. Picking up a heavy ironwood pestle, something like a club, he laid some of the bundled rice into the log and began pounding it. The steady rhythm of thump, thump, thump continued until he had pounded the husks off all the rice. Scraping the rice onto a flat basket, the boy flipped the basket in the air a number of times to let the wind blow the husks away. Now the rice was ready to cook for dinner.

As the missionaries and their carriers passed through the village, people stopped and stared at them. Some, who had learned a few words of English, called from their open doorways, "Where are you from?" "Why have you come?" "Where are you going?"

Most of these people had never been farther away than the next mountain, so Jo couldn't tell them they had come from California and had sailed 7,000 miles across the ocean. Instead, she just said, "We came from Manila, riding on a little bus for three days, and have been walking all day today from the end of the road."

The villagers pleasantly nodded and smiled in return.

Anne added, "Tomorrow we'll go on to Balangao. We want to live with the Balangao and learn their language so we can give them God's Word written in their language."

Fear gripped these mountain people when they heard the word *Balangao.* Jo and Anne remembered what Laurie had told them. The Balangao were enemies with many other head-hunting groups, especially the Ifugao (If'-uh-gow) people who lived a couple mountains over. Revenge killings ruled in their culture (One tribe would kill people in another tribe. That tribe would then take revenge and kill people in the first tribe). This put the Balangao in constant danger. Besides their enemies, the Balangao also lived in great fear of the spirits.

Jo and Anne had talked about the risk of living with headhunters, but had agreed that God called them to work among them. The Balangao were living and dying without knowing God. And Jo and Anne wanted them to know about God who has more power than all the spirits.

That night Jo and Anne rested their bone-weary bodies on the floor of the village school. As they settled down, Jo turned to Anne and said, "Did you get the feeling that today was just the beginning of explaining to people over and over why we've come? That always seems to be their main question."

Early the next morning the group began the last leg of their trek. It was late afternoon when Laurie shouted, "Jo and Anne, look! Down there in the midst of all those rice terraces, what do you see?"

Standing side by side, Jo and Anne caught their first glimpse of one of the Balangao villages. All their training and obedience in following the Lord step-by-step had led them to this.

Show Illustration #11

The next day Laurie took Jo and Anne from one Balangao village to another to meet people and ask about a house in which to live. People were nice everywhere they went, but they hadn't found the right house. The last village was Botac. This village had the best water supply which was close to the village. A family was building a new house and their current house would soon be empty. This, the women agreed, looked like a good place to live.

Canao (Kah-now'), an important Balangao leader, lived in Botac. Laurie had talked to him a few months before. Now he introduced Jo and Anne to him. Canao was small (he came only to Jo's shoulders) and he looked older than his about-fifty years. Life was difficult in these mountains. Many of Canao's teeth were missing. Those he did have were stained red from chewing the betel nut. (*Teacher:* Betel nuts are orange-colored nuts that grow on the betel palm. People in Southeast Asia chew the nuts.)

Laurie began the introductions. "Canao, I'm back! And I've brought the Americans you agreed to welcome and let live here. They're looking forward to living here in Botac and getting to know you."

Canao hid most of his shock. He shifted his bare feet in the dirt, looking with disbelief at Jo and Anne.

"Not women!" he exclaimed. "It's not safe for women to be here! Don't you know we're headhunters? I thought they'd be men. You brought women!"

Chapter 3
It Takes a Father

PRONUNCIATION GUIDE
Theser words are used in the text beneath Illustration #15:

Balangao Word	Phonetic Pronunciation
nokaychi	no-kaee-chee
apoy	ah-poy
pagey	pah-kuiy
mano	mah-no

Show Illustration #11

Evening seemed to descend quickly in the thickly forested mountain village. This was Jo and Anne's first evening with the Balangao people.

Canao, the respected Balangao leader, spoke. "The Americans will live in my nephew's house. It is a big room and has a separate cooking area. The water supply is just a five-minute walk over the terrace walls. We will get helpers to carry water." Turning to Jo and Anne he added, "And I want people to see you eating with us in our house."

Later Jo and Anne learned that when a Balangao feeds someone, it's his pledge to protect that one from any danger. By feeding them, Canao took a stand to protect the missionaries with his own life.

Dinner at Canao's that night was rice and boiled cabbage. After dinner Jo and Anne were escorted through the darkness with a burning torch to their own mountain home up on the next terrace. Their belongings had been carried up the ladder and stacked on the bamboo floor of their house on stilts.

Before settling down Jo and Anne talked into the night. "Canao seemed shocked that the Americans he agreed to have are women. I hope he's not too disappointed. Even as women we long to translate the Bible into Balangao. And besides, we feel sure God is the One who brought us here to the Balangao people."

Show Illustration #12

At daybreak, Jo and Anne went to separate corners in their new home. Spending an hour in their personal devotions by reading the Bible and praying had been their habit since high school days. After breakfast Anne started unpacking their supplies and settling into their house.

"Umphhhh," Anne groaned as she hoisted the box of canned goods onto the rafters for storage.

Aware that the Americans were awake, friendly and curious Balangao climbed the ladder to peer into the house. Because everyone knew what was inside each other's houses, some Balangao wanted to see what Jo and Anne put in their house, too.

One woman opened a cardboard box and announced to all the onlookers, "They have a *whole case* of laundry soap! Look!"

The Balangao couldn't understand why two American ladies would want to come live in their village of Botac. *Maybe they want to get our language and sell it in America. Maybe they cannot find jobs in America so came looking for work. Most likely they're looking for husbands since they don't have any!*

Canao supervised as Jo and Anne set up housekeeping. During one visit his usual smile had disappeared. He was extremely serious as he began, "As I told you, it is not really safe for women to be here in Balangao. We're headhunters and who knows what could happen." Jo and Anne listened in stunned silence. Canao continued, "You need someone to take care of you. I'll have to be your father."

Jo and Anne didn't know what to say. Neither of them really wanted a substitute father–an uncle maybe, but not a father. They could not see Canao as their *father*. But for Canao it was settled. He was their *FATHER*.

Laurie had remained in Balangao for several days to help Jo and Anne get settled. He constructed two beds and a table, then rigged up their two-way radio, their only contact with the outside world.

Jo tried it out. Holding the microphone close and calling to their organization's center of operations, a place that seemed another world away, she said, "Balangao, this is Balangao calling Manila."

For a few seconds they heard only scratchy, crackling noises from the speaker. Then Jo and Anne cheered when they finally heard "Manila to Balangao. Go ahead."

As the days passed, Anne said to Jo, "Every day here is an adventure! The Balangao ways are so different from the ways we grew up with in America."

One day Canao stopped by, "In a few days we're having an important Balangao gathering, a Peace Pact Celebration between us and a warring neighbor. I am inviting you ladies to come witness this by joining us at the celebration."

As Canao walked away, Jo said to Anne, "A peace pact. Humm. Isn't that where enemies come together and make a pact, promising not to kill each other and to allow the other to walk through their territory safely?"

"I'm thinking that would be a good thing here in this revenge-seeking area," said Anne. "Even if the pact gets broken some day, it should make life safer for all of us now."

Show Illustration #13

The Peace Pact gathering lasted through the night as the men talked. Now it was afternoon and the final celebration was to begin shortly. The village was packed with Balangao and the guests, their former enemies. The new pact was made and sung with a special type of song chant. Promises were chanted back and forth in song before hundreds of witnesses.

The colorful wraparound skirts worn by all the Balangao women caught Anne's eye. "We'll have to get one of those," she said. Jo and Anne had seen the village women weaving the skirts on their looms, each skirt made from a long piece of woven red, blue and white cloth.

Many of the tribal men, muscles rippling, squatted low to the ground on their haunches. They stood to chant and then joined the dances enthusiastically.

Jo pointed to one of the men who had a large tattoo all over his chest as she said to Anne, "Canao told me that when a Balangao has a chest tattoo like that it means he has taken a head."

Chills ran up and down Anne's back. She wondered, *Will giving these Balangao God's Word in their language help end the practice of headhunting?*

As Jo and Anne watched what was going on around them, Anne pointed to one man, "See the round brass thing that man is holding? I think they call it a gong. Its handle looks like a human jawbone to me."

Canao saw them looking at the gong. "That handle is the jaw-bone of a former enemy."

Jo and Anne shuddered to think of all those who had died in tribal wars. It was so sad. If only peace pacts could be made between all the mountain people groups and not be broken. If only they didn't insist on revenge.

Everyone listened as men from the two opposing tribes chanted many promises to each other.

Jo and Anne listened too. They'd been in Botac long enough to learn a lot of Balangao phrases. But the chants were hard to understand.

At the end of the day, after the peace pact was finished, Canao stood to his feet. As a respected Balangao leader, every eye was on him.

Canao boomed out his charge. (*Teacher:* For effect, repeat Canao's words aloud in a sing-song chanting style.) "These two ladies, Jo and Anne, are my daughters. They have eaten together

with us in our house, so just as we protect other Balangao we must also protect my two daughters from any harm." Then the gongs and dancing resumed. Every mountain person present knew that Canao would protect Jo and Anne with his life. Even Jo and Anne understood. Canao was their father, and if anything happened to them, he would take revenge!

As they feasted on boiled pig and cooked rice, Canao explained to Jo and Anne how people could now travel safely between these two areas with no worry of being attacked or killed unless the peace pact was broken. After the meal the gongs were brought out again. Canao said to Jo and Anne, "Now you, my daughters, join in the celebration. Dance with us."

Show Illustration #14

Jo looked at Anne. She knew there was no backing out of Canao's invitation. Half teasing, Jo said, "You go first. I'll follow."

Anne, always ready for adventure, called out over the gongs, "Come on, let's try! This looks like fun!"

Following the Balangao ladies, Jo and Anne awkwardly tried to match their foot movements on the hard-packed dirt with the fast rhythm of the gongs. They tried to extend their arms at just the right angle and follow the large circle of people in the dance until it ended.

Every star in the inky black sky above seemed to twinkle. Jo and Anne watched the crowd, group by group, leave for their villages. The lead person carried a torch of fire made from a bunch of long reeds. Each torch led a group of people into the dark night across the rice terrace trails.

In the dying light of the outdoor cooking fires, Canao approached Jo and Anne. Like a father trying to protect his daughters he cautioned, "From now on, when you travel outside of Balangao among other people, never tell them that you are from Balangao. You could be speaking to a person from an enemy group and not know it. If they knew you were living here they could take revenge on us Balangao by killing you."

Jo and Anne quickly agreed. "We will do what you say."

The two missionaries picked up their kerosene lantern, lit it and held it out in front of them as they followed others back over the rice terraces toward home. Reaching their house they did the customary "good-bye" saying, "We'll stop here; you go on ahead." Then they climbed up the ladder into their home.

"Let's take time to pray about what we've just seen and pray for all those we've met today," Anne suggested.

Jo agreed. "We're really going to need God's help and direction. There are so many good opportunities to share the Gospel if only we knew enough of the language." So they huddled close to the kerosene lamp, read the Bible together, and prayed for the people they had met, thanking God for all the experiences of the day.

Show Illustration #15

Opening her eyes, Jo squinted at her watch and said, "What's gotten into us, talking so late into the night?"

"It's all that strong black coffee we drank at the peace pact," Anne stated.

Jo was quiet for a moment and then she said, "Canao takes such good care of us. He protects us as if we were really his own daughters."

Anne added, "We'd be lost without his advice. He's spared us from making some terrible mistakes. He really is like a true father, isn't he? What's the Balangao word for father? *Ama* (Ah-mah)?"

"That's it," agreed Jo. "That's exactly what he is to us, a wonderful father. *Ama* Canao."

From then on Jo and Anne began calling Canao *Ama*.

One night Jo was reminiscing as they sat in their house. "Remember when we learned our most-used word in Balangao?" (*Teacher*: Consult pronunciation guide at beginning of chapter.)

"Yes, it was *nokaychi*," exclaimed Anne. "We've been asking *Nokaychi?* ("What is that?") over and over and over again!"

"*Nokaychi?*" Jo asked as she pointed to the flame that blazed inside their lantern.

"*Apoy*, fire." Anne got it right.

"*Nokaychi?*" Jo pointed to the bundles of drying rice.

"*Pagey*, rice," Anne quickly responded.

Jo tried to stump Anne. Pointing down through a hole in the floor to the chickens running loose under the house, "*Nokaychi?*"

"*Mano*, there are *mano* everywhere! Cluck, cluck, cluck." Then Anne continued, "Speaking of chickens, remember when we saw that little boy fall and injure himself outside our house? Then that evening an old woman came with a live chicken in her hands. Holding it by its feet she swung it 'round and 'round in the air calling out the injured child's name over and over. She was trying to call back the boy's soul so he wouldn't get sick and die."

"I remember that," Jo chimed in. "And remember the other time when we asked that Balangao lady the name of her mother-in-law? She wouldn't tell us. Finally, she leaned over to a friend and said, 'You say her name.' That friend explained to us that Balangao people believe they will break out with bad sores (boils) if they say the name of their mother-in-law."

Each new sentence seemed to begin with *remember*. Jo and Anne soon realized how much God had helped and cared for them in those first days in Balangao.

Then sounding somewhat wistful, Jo said, "Won't it be wonderful when God helps us speak Balangao with ease, sounding like they do? I long for the day when I can pray in the Balangao language without searching and searching for the right Balangao words to say."

Anne stretched and said sleepily, "At least we're talking some Balangao. It's coming more easily now. And *Ama* Canao, our father, was right when he told us, 'If you would just eat more rice, you ladies could speak Balangao better.' We're eating lots of meals with Balangao now, and it's true, our Balangao language is improving!"

With that, Anne tossed her blond head back on her pillow and fell asleep.

But sleep was not quick in coming to Jo. Her thoughts began to drift. She thought about how Anne's doctor father had died when Anne was just a teenager. Then she thought about her own dad back at home on their California farm. Then her thoughts came back to *Ama* Canao and how he treated them as if he *were* their father. He had been the one to find them a place to stay by telling his niece and her husband, Tekla and Tony, to move early into their still-being-built house so Jo and Anne could move into their old one. And Jo's thoughts jumped to Tekla who had become like a sister to them. They longed for her to come to know the Lord. "Lord, please draw Tekla to yourself," Jo prayed as sleep finally came.

Chapter 4
Harvest Begins–Tekla and Ama

A NOTE TO THE TEACHER

Chapter 4 is written in two parts. If you have 30 minutes for storytelling, you will be able to tell both Parts 1 and 2. If you have a shorter storytelling time, tell just Part 1 or Part 2 since both parts may be told independently of each other.

If you do not teach Part 1, add this brief statement near the end of Part 2: "Prior to Canao's conversion, Tekla, one of Jo and Anne's Balangao language helpers, became the first believer among the Balangao. God heard her sincere longing to know Him and sent Jo and Anne to tell her about Jesus."

If you do not teach Part 2, add this brief statement near the end of Part 1: "As Canao worked with Jo and Anne to translate the Bible into the Balangao language, he came to see the truth of God's Word and placed his trust in Jesus Christ. Canao was filled with great joy when the Ifugao, once the fiercest enemies of the Balangao, invited him to baptize their first Christian believers."

PART 1—TEKLA

Jo sighed as she spoke to Anne. "I think absolutely everyone of these Balangao people obey the spirit mediums, like Forsan (For-sahn), Chalinggay (Chu-ling-kooy), and Uyyama (Ooy-yah-ma)."

"All?" Anne questioned. "Not Tekla, the daughter of Uyyama. Uyyama, the most powerful spirit medium in all the area, tells stories of how their family is descended from a spirit that lives in his house. Remember how Tekla told us she stopped sacrificing to the spirits because she wanted to know God? And she told us how the spirits always scared her, trying to frighten her back into sacrificing to them. Before she believed, they even started appearing to her and she kept trying to run away."

Show Illustration #16

"You're right," Jo responded. "I was helping Tekla pick beans in her garden one afternoon. She told me that just before we came to live in Balangao, she'd suffered so much that she had almost given up her search for God. She thought she could never know Him. She was nearly ready to sacrifice again to the spirits. Then we came and she never stops asking questions. She *loves* to hear about the Lord Jesus and keeps saying, 'I *wish* I could know God.'"

Just then Tekla arrived at Jo and Anne's door to help them. She was determined to teach them her language well. She worked steadily throughout the day helping the ladies figure out an alphabet for Balangao.

By late afternoon Tekla stood to stretch. "The sun is setting; I must go home and cook our rice for tonight." Long, lean shadows followed Tekla as she scurried across the terraces to her house by the bamboo water pipe.

Throughout the village the rhythmic thumping of rice being pounded was heard. Soon it would be cooking in large aluminum rice pots. The Balangao lived on the rice they grew and harvested themselves. The very name of their village, Botac, meant "harvest."

But another kind of "harvest" was on Jo's mind. "Anne, the rice granaries here may be full, but I wish the Balangao knew the food that lasts longer than rice, the food of God's Word. No one here is a believer yet. Until Jesus, the Lord of the harvest, becomes Lord of the Balangao, not even part of our work is done." (*Teacher:* See Luke 10:2.)

Anne reminded Jo, "It will not be an easy harvest to gather. Tekla's father, Uyyama, holds much power as a spirit medium in all of Balangao. For years he's been caretaker of the *toeto* (tow-ey-tow) spirit who lives in a bamboo tube inside that clay pot hanging from the rafters of his house. The *toeto* speaks on its own to Uyyama."

The thought of the *toeto*, a talking spirit living in a bamboo tube, gave Jo goose bumps. This wasn't make-believe, like in a fairy tale book or a movie. Anne continued, "Remember that Tekla told us how her father, Uyyama, in desperation, agreed to be the servant of the *toeto?* It was after six of his seven children had died."

"Yes," Jo said with sadness in her voice. "Only his daughter Tekla was left alive. To keep this last child alive Uyyama agreed to become the servant and keeper of the *toeto* spirit. That's why he obeys it. It's so easy to get discouraged by the hold that the spirits have on the Balangao. But God's Word tells us the fields are white for harvest, so we need to pray faithfully for Tekla so she can know God."

Jo and Anne stopped and prayed for Tekla. "Dear Lord, we praise You that Tekla continually refuses to sacrifice to the evil spirits and obey them. She longs to know You. Please help her to understand Your Word, the Bible. Help her to realize that You are more powerful than the spirits. In Jesus' name we pray. Amen."

As the Bible translation team progressed, Jo and Anne kept learning more Balangao words and sentences from Tekla. And Tekla kept learning more of God's Word from Jo and Anne. She loved hearing the stories of Jesus: His miracles, His death, and His resurrection. And Tekla longed for the day she could read all those stories in her own language, in her very own Balangao New Testament.

Show Illustration #17

One morning as the three women worked together, Jo asked, "Tekla, that is a beautiful beaded necklace. Did your mother give it to you?"

"Yes," Tekla said as she let it slide through her fingers. "It is my inheritance. I treasure it."

Jo continued, "In Jesus' day, women received a necklace of very expensive coins on their wedding day. They wore them around the top of their head."

"She wore *money* in her hair?" Tekla laughed as she thought how it would have looked to wear coins in her hair!

Jo continued the Bible story. "Jesus told of a woman who lost one of her 10 coins from the necklace she'd been given on her wedding day."

"Oh no!" Tekla gasped. "What did she do about it?"

Anne answered, "She did exactly what you would do if you lost one of the beads in your inherited necklace. She lit a lantern, moved everything in the house, and carefully swept the floor in search of the coin."

With emotion Tekla burst out, "I would have even searched under the house to be sure the chickens did not get it. Did the lady find her coin?"

"Yes, she did," Jo said with a big smile. "And she was *so* happy. Tekla, that story Jesus told is about us. We're like that lost coin. We are loved and treasured by God. But sin separates us from Him. It's like we're lost. Just as that lady in the story did everything she could to find the lost coin, God has done everything necessary to 'find' us. He sent Jesus, His only Son, to die on the cross in our place to pay for our sins so that we can be clean before God. Jesus died, but then He rose again! He's alive and He loves us!"

Tekla thought about Jesus all year long. She kept asking questions, learning. Then, one spring day, after hearing and hearing God's Word for months, she understood. And like the lost coin, Tekla was "found" by God.

Jo and Anne rejoiced when Tekla came and told them, "How *different* my life is since God has come to me. I talk to Him directly, I tell Him my fears, and He is my protector. He is not like the evil spirits. He does not lie. I can trust Him."

God's harvest was beginning in Botac!

PART 2—AMA

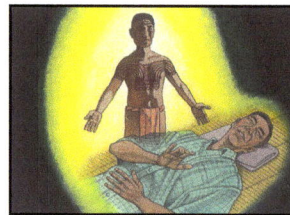

Show Illustration #18

It was the middle of the night in Botac. Ama suddenly sat straight up on his woven reed mat. He'd been awakened by a puzzling dream in which a man, dressed like a Balangao, appeared to him. But he was a Balangao that Ama had never met.

Ama asked the stranger, "*Why* have these American children, Jo and Anne, *really* come here to Balangao?"

The stranger spoke like a man of great wisdom and said, "Your American children have come to tell you something that is more enduring than a great, mighty rock. Believe what they tell you." And suddenly Ama woke up.

Unable to sleep, Ama wrapped his arms around his knees, as he kept thinking and thinking about that dream. *What does it mean? What did that stranger mean when he said Jo and Anne have a message for me that will last longer than a great, mighty rock? What could possibly last longer than a rock? Rocks never seem to change, even the ones in the river where water keeps flowing over them. People change. We live and die, but rocks are always the same.*

Ama determined in his mind, *I will try to listen more carefully to my American children. I wonder what kind of ancient truth they have brought to us?* Then he lay back and slept the remainder of the night.

For years Ama never told Jo about his dream. But the stranger's words made Ama listen carefully to what the Bible had to say. Not knowing this, Jo sometimes wondered if Ama would ever believe.

Not long after Ama's dream Anne told Jo, "Tom has asked me to marry him and I said 'yes.' I will return to the USA to marry him." Jo was happy that Anne was going to marry her lifelong friend, but now she would be alone in Balangao.

After Anne left, Ama, like a good father, became very concerned about Jo. The very next day after Anne left he told Jo, "You will be lonely without Anne. I am afraid that when you get lonely, you will want to go back to America, too, leaving us alone. From now on you must eat all your meals at our house with us." So Jo began eating all her meals with different Balangao families.

At one evening meal, as Jo sat on the floor with Ama's family, the plates of dished-up rice were placed before them. Ina, Jo's Balangao mother, took a pot off the cooking fire behind her and began dishing up its contents into bowls.

They passed a bowl to Jo. It was full of roasted, creepy, big-bodied beetle bugs!

Fifteen-year-old Doming and four-year-old Celia loved Jo like a big sister. Delighted at the treat on their plates they exclaimed, "Roasted beetles are a special Balangao food. You will like them. Try some!"

Jo couldn't bear to offend the family. Ina always tried so hard to have something to eat along with their rice, but this time of year extra food was hard to find. Jo didn't want anyone to see her cringe, but she wondered, *How will I ever eat a roasted beetle?* Her voice a bit squeaky, she said to Celia, "But I don't know how to eat these . . . ."

Happily, Celia picked up a big fat beetle. It filled her small hand. Then she demonstrated, "Just pull off the legs and remove the sticker like this." With that Celia popped the bug into her mouth and crunched down on it.

Cautiously, Jo did the same. "Hmm. Not too bad. It crunches like . . . potato chips." Everyone laughed as Jo reached for another beetle.

Jo and Anne had taught Ama how to read his own language long before they had completed the Balangao reading books. After Anne left to get married, Jo continued translating with the Balangao. One day while helping Jo with translation, Ama reached for her English New Testament. He started scanning the verses on the first page, Matthew chapter one.

Suddenly Ama exclaimed, "You . . . you mean this Book has a list of ancestors? The actual names of the world's first people?"

"Yes, you're looking at the genealogy of Jesus Christ," Jo said to Ama. "It goes back to the early people on earth."

Jo, still not realizing how important the list of names was to Ama, continued, "But those are just names. Why not skip over those names and get to the pages beyond where the good stories are."

But Ama didn't skip ahead. He was too overwhelmed by the list of names. "You mean this Book is true? These are the actual names of the people?" For the Balangao, having the actual names of the people was proof that the Bible was really a true story, a record, and not just make-believe.

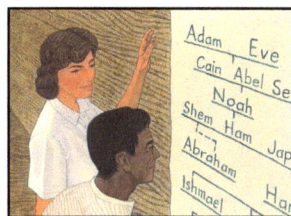

Show Illustration #19

Jo finally understood. The genealogy was very important to Ama. She got a long piece of shelf paper, hung it on the wall and began writing the names on it from the Bible, starting with Adam and Eve right down to Jesus. Soon the names stretched from ceiling to floor.

Ama studied the chart, then carefully removed it from the wall. He took it with him down into the village to show to people.

He took the list everywhere! He took it to people's houses and to village meetings, explaining the story to everyone he met. Ama told the people, "We always thought that the banana plant and the rock had argued about who would give birth to human beings. Our ancestors told us that somehow the banana plant defeated the rock and that's why people are just like the banana plant: they are born, grow up, produce shoots (children), get old, and die. People would have lived forever if only the rock would have won the argument. We have believed that, but have never known the names of the banana plant's descendents. But look! This Book that Jo is putting into our language has the *actual names* of the first people on earth written down in it! That proves this Book is true!"

Jo was astonished. *The list of Bible names was the key that began to unlock Ama's heart!* The Book was bringing a harvest in Balangao, one person at a time.

Six years had passed since Jo had first arrived in Balangao and started living there. She and her team finished translating the books of Mark and First John.

She'd witnessed to Ama, but somehow he was still resistant. Handing the typed pages of 1 John to Ama, Jo requested, "Would you please check the grammar?"

Ama's eyes widened as he read. "My child, these words are *good*! People would believe this if they could just hear it!"

Jo was caught by surprise. She'd been trying to tell these things to him for six years! But hiding her surprise she said, "What shall we do so people can hear it?"

Ama didn't answer.

But that night he and a group of Balangao showed up at Jo's house and sat down on the floor (as Balangao always did). Ama spoke, "Here we are. We have come to hear the words of that Book; teach us."

Jo was bewildered. They'd never listened like this before. She had told them over and over about God, about Jesus and about how to get their sins forgiven. So haltingly she asked, "Teach you what?" It was only later that Jo realized that in Balangao, younger people cannot teach older people, and Jo was younger. They must ask you questions. Older ones just won't listen unless they ask about a matter.

Show Illustration #20

The dozen or so Balangao started to ask question after question. "If this religion is so good, do you know where people came from?" "Why is there trouble in the world?" "Why do our children get sick and die?" "If God is stronger than Satan, why doesn't He get rid of him?" They kept asking all kinds of questions because they wanted to know more about this Creator God.

As time passed, Jo wondered what was really happening in the hearts of the Balangao. Ama helped her to understand. "Jo, my child, by asking questions these people are coming closer to understanding the Truth just as I did."

Sunday after Sunday they gathered to study the Bible and to find answers to their questions. As they believed, Jo wanted the Christian Balangao men who helped translate every day to teach on Sunday, especially when she wasn't there. But they wouldn't. Jo was always the one to teach. She tried everything she knew to convince them to teach. They were capable, but they still wouldn't. They said they didn't know enough about God and what if they couldn't answer people's questions.

Jo was now translating the book of 1 Timothy with Ama. There in chapter two, verse twelve, Paul wrote to Timothy that he does not allow women to teach men. Ama didn't say anything to Jo, but that next Sunday morning, before Jo could stand and begin teaching, Ama stood up and announced, "My daughter here knows more about God and His Word than I do. But we found in the Bible that women are not supposed to teach men. So I guess I have to be the one." That was when the Balangao started teaching God's Word.

From that Sunday on, with Jo's help, Ama and other believing Balangao men began leading the Sunday Bible studies. Soon the Balangao church grew to 60 and on up to 200 and more. Person after person "faced God," the Balangao way of explaining how a person comes to know Jesus as their Saviour. They were now taking God's advice from the Bible, turning away from obeying the evil spirits.

Ama was filled with great joy when the Ifugao, once the fiercest enemies of the Balangao, invited him to baptize their first Christian believers.

Jo, the shy farm girl from California, watched Ama believe the creation story from God's Word, then place his trust in the Creator's Son, Jesus. The harvest began in Botac and continued throughout the region as Ama took the good news of Jesus even into enemy territory.

NOTE TO THE TEACHER

The Truth is what God says, and the Bible is God's complete revelation. We do not advocate that Christians rely on dreams to discover additional truth. But many missionaries in similar situations, such as Jo and Anne's, report that especially before people receive the Scriptures in their own language, God, not uncommonly, seems to use dreams as a means to prepare that person to receive the Truth. In Bible times God used dreams to give warnings to unbelievers (Genesis 41:15; Daniel 2:1-2), to instruct (Matthew 2:12), etc. But those dreams tended to cease when the Scriptures came. It appears that God used Ama's dream to get through to this very influential Balangao man. Ama's dream did not bring him to salvation in Christ. Ama still had to hear God's Word and act upon its truth to become a believer. Joanne Shetler and thousands of Wycliffe missionaries give the best years of their lives in remote places around the world to make God's truth available for those who have never heard. Romans 10:17 reminds us that faith can come when a person hears the Word of God.

Chapter 5
The Crash, The Cries, The Celebration

Show Illustration #21

Every month Jo flew south from her mountain home to Wycliffe Bible Translators' Center in Bagabag (Bah-gah'-bahg). From her small cottage in Bagabag, she typed letters to praying friends in the USA. Over the nine years she'd been a missionary in the Philippines, she'd filled her missionary letters with details, stories and photos of her Balangao family.

On April 15, 1971, Jo's fingers flew over the keys as she typed a letter to those praying for her at home. She asked them to imagine 70 Balangao adults squashed into her one-room (10' x 18') home every Sunday from almost 9 a.m. to noon or later. She wrote, "Sometimes there are so many people the overflow crowd has to stand outside to listen."

In her letter she was asking for prayer for the Balangao as they cut and gathered trees from the forest and sawed them into boards to build a church. A bigger building was needed desperately to hold all the people. On Wednesday evenings believers gathered to study God's Word, on Thursday nights the kids came for Bible stories, and on Friday evenings Jo helped the men prepare to teach God's Word on Sundays.

Pausing as she wrote, Jo wondered if she should write what really troubled her. Her heart was aching for the Balangao because they didn't seem to really understand about praying. She had asked God to make them a people of prayer. They had excellent reasoning abilities, but they didn't talk to God about their thoughts and plans. They forgot to ask God for wisdom to do things His way. Jo longed for them to depend more on God.

Jo had been waking in the night and often prayed: *Dear Lord, please teach these Balangao believers how to really pray. They like to hear me pray, but they won't pray on their own. How can they really know You?* Then one day when things got overwhelming, in desperation she'd prayed: *Lord, I don't care what You have to do. Please teach these Balangao how to pray. Do something, just make them pray!* Jo paused. Should she share these thoughts? She continued typing her letter: "This brings me to the very 'meat of my need.' If ever you prayed for Balangao, pray for us now."

Glancing at the clock Jo jumped up from her desk. *It's nearly time for the helicopter to arrive out at the airstripI'll finish writing this later when I return.*

Across the field at the Bagabag airstrip Jo greeted Dr. Lim, the Filipino doctor who was coming to Balangao in order to build a clinic there. He'd arranged for a large U.S. Marine military helicopter to fly tons of building materials into Balangao: bags of cement, nails and roofing.

Missionary pilot Bill Powell was going along to direct the American pilots over the mountains to Balangao. He'd flown into Balangao territory countless times and knew the area well. Jo was invited to fly along as interpreter for the American pilots. She invited her Balangao "brother," Doming, Ama's son, to come along since he was on his way home for college break. It would be a free ride!

The helicopter loaded, Jo climbed in and sat on top of the 10 tons of bagged cement. She looked at Doming standing inside by the chopper window. She had long prayed for this young brother of hers. *Father, thank You that Doming has come to know You as Saviour. But it's been 11 months, and he's still struggling about giving his life completely to You. Please, capture his love.*

As the engines roared to life, the swirling chopper blades hesitantly lifted the helicopter. Jo watched Dr. Lim who could barely control his excitement. She remembered how God had worked in this young doctor's life so that he would give up a successful medical career to come to a remote area like Balangao. *God, You have given him a special gift for medicine and I'm so thankful he wants to use it in Balangao where the people desperately need medical helHis coming will also free me to focus on translating Your Word.*

Slowly the "Jolly Green Giant" helicopter lumbered into the sky with its heavy load, heading north over valleys and mountains below. Thirty minutes later they were circling over the main village of Balangao, an hour up the mountain from Botac.

Bill pointed toward the school playground, directing the military pilots, "You can set it down over there."

They began to descend. Suddenly something went terribly wrong. The mountains seemed to close in. The chopper was losing altitude. It was doing down! The pilots couldn't control it! Slash! The spinning rotor blades sheered off the top of a betel nut tree. Branches flew through the air. Then the helicopter hit the mountain, flipped on its side and plunged into a deep ravine.

The engines were running at top speed. Spinning blades chopped and pounded the ground, shaking the helicopter violently. Quickly all four blades splintered, and pieces went spinning through the air into the rice fields.

Tons of cargo was thrown around, burying the passengers. The bags of cement were torn open and clouds of cement dust engulfed everything and everyone trapped inside.

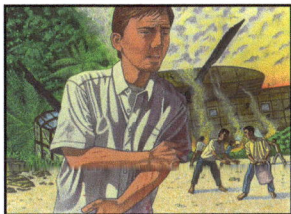

Show Illustration #22

Bill, though badly injured, jammed his fist through the cockpit window and scrambled out, the flight crew following right behind him. Pulling himself up the embankment he moaned, horror gripping him, "Oh, no! Dear God, help . . . fire!"

Both of the choppers' rotor hubs were on fire and fuel was gushing out into the creek bed!

The military pilots, realizing the fire danger, yelled at the Balangao gathered on the bank, "Run! Run! It's going to explode!" Everyone turned to run.

But Bill shouted to the Balangao, "Wait! Jo, Doming and Dr. Lim are still inside!"

Immediately the Balangao turned and ran back to the burning helicopter. Grabbing any container around, they all started throwing pails, pans and pots full of water. They scooped up mud from the rice fields and threw it on the flames. When they finally got the fires out, some Balangao men scrambled down the bank and hoisted themselves up into the chopper. Digging through the cargo and throwing kegs of nails and bags of cement out of the helicopter, they tried to find Jo, Doming and Dr. Lim.

Buried upside down under broken bags of cement, Jo regained consciousness and pleaded with God: *I can't die yet. Who will finish the translation if I die?* Finally she felt the rescuers walking on top of her. But she couldn't move.

Cement dust flew as men dug through the cargo. Then one stopped. "Listen! Under here. I think I hear the sound of a cat down below!" It was Jo's muffled voice as she, with all her might, tried to call out, "*Antoyan-ani.* Here we are!"

The men dug furiously. "Here are her feet!" They pulled hard. But Jo was crammed in so tightly they couldn't budge her. "Dig more!" they shouted to one another.

When they freed Jo from the rubble, she was gasping for air. Somehow they hoisted her out of the helicopter and carried her up the embankment to the safety of a nearby building.

Other Balangao found Doming and then Dr. Lim and pulled them out of the wreck. Now everyone was out.

Lying on the floor, covered from head to toe with white cement powder and surrounded by Balangao, Jo was in terrible pain. She barely noticed her broken ribs, broken collarbone, collapsed lung, massive bruises and several bleeding gashes. It was the cement powder which had filled her eyes when she'd been unconscious that gave unbearable pain. (*Teacher:* One of the ingredients in cement is lime. It becomes even more caustic when mixed with water. Yet, there was no other way to wash the cement powder away but to pour water into Jo's eyes. It's actually caustic without water. Handling the powder can finally blister one's hands.)

Within minutes Jo's neck became so swollen that she couldn't move her head. She gasped for every breath. *My eyes feel like they are on fire,* Jo agonized. Using all the strength she could muster, Jo pleaded with the Balangao women crowded around her. "Pour water into my eyes. Keep pouring it in. Wash out the cement."

The searing pain of the cement in her eyes was only intensified by the water. It felt as if hot embers of a fire were being held on her eyes.

Try as she might, Jo couldn't see anything out of her eyes. Faintly, she croaked out again, "Keep pouring water in my eyes no matter how much it hurts me. Don't stop."

Hour after hour the Balangao women washed out Jo's eyes. Now her prayer was: *Lord, I can't be blind! How will I finish the translation?*

Meanwhile people raced down the mountain to Botac shouting to Ama and Tekla about the fiery crash.

Ama dropped his axe, ran an hour barefoot up the mountain toward the crash site. He talked to God as he ran, *Oh, dear Lord, what happened to Job is what has happened to me. My oldest son and my American daughter are both gone in a single night.*

When Tekla heard, she raced up the steep mountain, too. But pounding in her ears all the way up the mountain, like a recording she couldn't erase, were the constant warnings of the unbelievers. From the first day Tekla started working on Bible translation with Jo and Anne, she'd endured these warnings: *God will punish you! God will punish you! You are polluting His holy Word by putting it into our lowly Balangao language. God will punish you.*

Breathless, Tekla reached the top of the mountain and crumbled under a tree. Praying as she'd never prayed before, she cried out, *Oh, holy God, it's up to You. If we have truly polluted Your holy Word by putting it in our lowly language, we accept Your punishment, and Jo will die. But God, if You really want Your holy Word in our lowly language, let Jo live. But God, I need a sign.*

Then, with faith that could move a mountain, Tekla prayed, *If I say her name, "Jo," and she answers back with my name, "Tekla," I will know that she will live. And I'll know that You want Your holy Word in our lowly language.*

Tekla jumped up and raced to the building where Jo lay stretched out on the floor. She shouted, "Jo! Jo!"

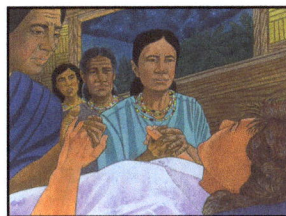

Show Illustration #23

Jo's voice was barely audible, "Tekla, Tekla, it's okay . . . I'll be okay."

Beyond belief, Tekla shouted, "She is going to live! She is going to live!"

The Balangao women standing all around Jo tried to hush Tekla. "What is wrong with you? Can't you see? She is already dead; it is just her voice that is left!"

But Tekla *knew* differently. Her faith in God soared! "God will keep her alive. She will be all right. You will see!" And

Tekla fell on her knees beside Jo, pleading, "Jo, tell me what to do for you."

Jo, trained in missionary medicine and survival, knew she was going into shock. "Prop up my feet; get me some strong coffee to drink; cover me with blankets. But DON'T stop washing the cement out of my eyes."

As the night hours passed, Jo overheard snatches of conversations in the background. "Doming and the pilot, Bill, are injured, but they survived." Relief swept over Jo. But toward morning Jo learned that Dr. Lim's injuries had been too great: he lived only until midnight.

Little did Jo know that earlier, as Doming lay helplessly under piles of rubble in the downed helicopter, he was doing some serious praying, too, finally submitting to what God wanted. *God, if You let me live, I will serve You forever, no matter how hard it is.*

Throughout the night, one after another, the Balangao Christians arrived. They crowded around Jo, and all on their own, one after another, they prayed earnestly. And their prayer was: "God, do not let her die yet; the Book is not finished!"

As Jo listened to them praying, even in great pain she was amazed at what God was doing. She felt immense joy when she remembered her prayer: *Lord, I don't care what it takes; please make these people pray! Do anything it takes.* Maybe this crash was part of the "anything."

The crash marked the beginning of the Balangao's *talking to God about everything.*

Now they knew they couldn't depend just on their hard work and wits. They needed God and His hel(*Teacher:* See Proverbs 21:31.)

Jo's sight was fully restored, and Doming lived to keep his promise to the Lord. He sacrificed by taking a year off from college to help Jo finish the Balangao translation.

Nine days before Christmas 1981, the translation team finished the New Testament in Balangao. At last the Book was done! It was almost twenty years since Jo had come to the Philippines.

In July 1982 just four days before one of the biggest events ever to be held in Botac–the dedication of the Balangao New Testament–a monstrous typhoon (hurricane) hit! Torrents of rain poured out of the black sky. Trails became slick and nearly impassable. Winds tore at the thatched homes.

For two days the typhoon raged. Then suddenly, contrary to all expectation, sunshine broke through! Someone from a nearby village looked at the clear sky and exclaimed, "How could the typhoon be over so suddenly? Oh, yes, it is because it is time for the dedication of the Balangao New Testament. Those people have power with God!"

Show Illustration #24

On July 24 and 25 a thousand people gathered to dedicate the Balangao New Testament. Celebrating and rejoicing, they played gongs, wrote special songs, sang and told stories about how God's Word had helped them. All took place on the mountainside below their church as they sat under the shade of coconut palm leaves woven together. Anybody who wanted could speak.

Tekla walked to the microphone. Stillness settled over the crowd as she told about the night of the helicopter crash. She told how people were afraid at first to put the Word of God into a lowly language like Balangao. "People kept warning us that God would punish us because we were desecrating His holy Word." And she told them how God had confirmed to her that He wanted His Word in their language.

As was fitting, Ama led in all the events of the two-day celebration. Jo honored him with the first printed Balangao New Testament. Holding the Book high, he shouted, "*THIS* is what we have been waiting for!" He spoke through tears of joy. "God has been merciful to let me live to see this day." Cheers rose from the happy crowd.

Masa-aw told the audience, "Long ago, I didn't have any interest in God. My ears were shut to why the missionaries had really come. But they invited me to come to their house and 'just talk to us anyway.' So I would go to Jo and Anne's house. And as I began to hear the Word of God, I found there was no place to hide from the Truth of this Book. Then one day I said, 'God, take me, I am Yours.' I give thanks that we have this Book. This Book speaks Balangao. We must follow it. This Book is now our Teacher."

Twenty years after moving into this remote area of the northern Philippines and serving as a Wycliffe Bible Translator, Jo Shetler, a happy missionary, could look back at all that God had done. Once just a shy farm girl who wanted to do something that would last forever, her prayer had been answered! And a people were forever changed by the Book. The Balangao still follow the Book. The Book's truth, as Ama learned, is more enduring than the mighty rock. That's the way of the Book! Has it changed you?

EPILOGUE

(*Teacher:* Tell this section of the story if time allows. If not, then use this information to answer questions children might have.)

Ten months after the celebration of the New Testament dedication, while Jo was in the States visiting all the Christians who prayed and gave to her work, Ama became ill. Ama had always worried about what would happen if he had "unconfessed sin" in his life when he died. Jo had told him, "The best thing is to always confess sin when it happens." And then she'd prayed with him that God would allow him to confess his sin before he took his last breath.

Now, very ill, Ama prayed throughout the night. His family spent the night by his side. Then toward morning, propped up on his sleeping mat, Ama was satisfied and spoke right out loud to the Lord, "It is okay; You can take me now, Lord Jesus." Ama closed his eyes to earth and entered into Heaven. At that very moment a large earthquake shook the entire region.

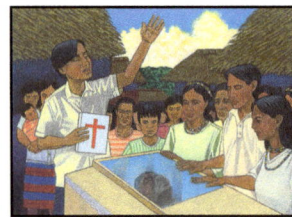

Show Illustration #25

News of Ama's death spread quickly. The Balangao all said, "It was Ama Canao stepping into Heaven that shook the earth." Over 400 people hiked to the far place where Ama had died. Out of love and respect for their beloved friend, their long, long procession carried his body all the way back to Botac.

The village was packed with people from many places, all coming to share their sadness and yet rejoice that Ama was with his Saviour, Jesus Christ. For it was Ama who had told many of those hundreds of people how to "face God" and know Jesus Christ as Saviour.

Ama's son, Doming, taught day and night at his father's wake, reading from Ama's Balangao New Testament. "The Book tells us that believers will live again because Christ did. Jesus was the first to be raised from the dead, and we will all follow." Speaking over Ama's grave, Doming told the crowds,

"This is only my father's body that will be buried. Ama is with the Lord."

Back in the U. S., Jo had a difficult time at first accepting Ama's death. But when she learned how the Lord had helped Ama as he died, and how God shook the earth upon Ama's arrival in Heaven, she was able to let him go. She could rejoice, too, at how God was honored at Ama's funeral. Joy and hope filled her heart for Ama who was now with his Saviour.

On June 11, 2004, Ina, Jo's Balangao mother, joined Ama in Heaven.

After 20 years of living in her mountain home in Balangao, Jo moved to Wycliffe's Translation Center in Bagabag (nearly 60 miles away, a 21-minute flight). There she worked to prepare other Bible translation teams who, like her, were sent to places just like Balangao. Presently, Jo lives in the United States, yet returns to visit her beloved Balangao family and is working with them to translate the Old Testament.

Review Questions

Chapter 1

1. What difficult job did Jo Shetler's father ask her to do while he was out in the field? *("Just do it Jo! Get in the truck and drive it to me!")*

2. Why did Jo unwrap her brother's candy bar, eat it, then stuff the empty candy bar with paper? *(She was trying to play a joke on him to get even with him for being a bully.)*

3. The Shetler family were not churchgoers, but what special church program did Pastor Brown invite Jo, Wayne and Art to attend? *(An after-school kid's meeting at the church to hear and see a Gospel magician)*

4. Why do you think Pastor Brown invited the Shetler kids to hear the Gospel magician? *(He wanted Jo, Wayne and Art to hear the good news about Jesus.)*

5. Which of the Gospel magician's colored scarves told about a loving God and His beautiful home, Heaven? *(Gold)*

6. What did the Gospel magician tell the children about the red scarf? *(The wonderful news that God sent His Son Jesus who died on the cross in their place for their sins)*

7. Why did Heaven sound like a special place to Jo? *(There was a lot of trouble and anger on earth but not in Heaven.)*

8. What was the "best news" that Jo ever heard? *(That God loved her, wanted to forgive her sins and give her eternal life)*

9. What did Jo do about the "best news" she'd ever heard? *(She "JUST DID IT"–believed and asked Jesus to be her Saviour!)*

10. Just as the Gospel magician told Jo and the other kids, what will help you grow (green scarf) to become a stronger follower of Jesus? *(Read the Bible, talk to God, listen to people teach from the Bible, and obey God.)*

Chapter 2

1. Complete this sentence: Jo always wanted to do something with her life that would last _____. *(Forever)*

2. Please describe what Jo meant by: "I want to do something with my life that will last forever." *(If she worked as a nurse, her patients might get well but would eventually die. But as a missionary, she could help others to know Jesus as Saviour. That would bring eternal life to the person, and her work would last forever.)*

3. After high school graduation Jo studied in various schools in preparation to be a missionary. Can you name one or all three schools? *(Bible college, Jungle Survival School, SIL–Summer Institute of Linguistics.)*

4. Why did Jo decide to become a Bible translator? *(She understood that translating God's Word into the heart language of Bibleless people would allow them to hear the good news of Jesus. And Bible translation was doing something that would "last forever" because God's Word lasts forever.)*

5. What was the good advice about prayer that a missionary speaker gave to Jo? How would her prayer have sounded? *(The advice was: "Now, as a young person, begin to pray for the people that God will send you to." Jo's prayer may have sounded like this: "Lord, I don't know where I am going to be a missionary someday. But right now begin to prepare the hearts of those that I will teach. Help them to understand and accept the good news of Jesus.")*

6. To what country did God send Jo and Anne to work as missionary Bible translators? *(The Philippines)*

7. Name the group of Filipino people with whom Jo and Anne lived in the mountain village of Botac? *(The Balangao)*

8. What was the name of the Balangao leader? What was his reaction when he was introduced to Jo and Anne? *(Camao. "It's not safe for women to live here! We're headhunters!")*

9. How would you have reacted to Camao's words if you had been Jo and Anne? *(Allow varied responses which could lead to an excellent discussion about what to do with fear, how to trust that God didn't make a mistake, etc.)*

10. If God showed you that He wanted you to be a missionary, name a country where you would like to take the good news of Jesus. *(Allow class to list any countries they wish.)*

Chapter 3

1. What Balangao word did Jo and Anne constantly repeat while learning the Balangao language? What does it mean? *(Nokaychi, meaning "what is it?" Teacher: Help students to see that all language is learned by asking "What is it?" Demonstrate by pointing to a chair and asking "What is it?" Ask class to shout the answer. Repeat activity to demonstrate language acquisition.)*

2. What did Canao mean when he insisted that Jo and Anne "eat at his house"? *(He was pledging to protect the missionaries from danger.)*

3. What good morning habit did Jo and Anne begin in high school and continue when they shared a home in Botac? *(They each read the Bible, prayed and had personal devotions.)*

4. Why would Jo and Anne's habit of Bible reading and prayer be good for you? *(Get to know God's Word better;*

enjoy talking with God. Teacher: *Suggest using the word ACTS to help them pray: A–Adore God, tell Him how great He is. C–Confess your sins by saying you are sorry and need His help to live right. T–Thank God for everything He has done each day. S–Supplication, pray for others.)*

5. Why did Canao say that he would be Jo and Anne's "father"? *(As the respected leader of the Balangao, Canao was protecting the missionaries with his life as a father would do. It was his way of warning warring neighbors not to dare harm his daughters/the missionaries.)*

6. What was the Balangao "good-bye" that Jo and Anne said when they arrived at their home following the peace pact fire? *("We'll stop here; you go on ahead.")*

7. What new name did Jo and Anne give Canao? *(Ama, the Balangao word for "father.")*

8. Why did Jo and Anne work hard to learn and speak Balangao? *(They wanted to pray in Balangao without needing to search for the right words. And they especially wanted to share the good news of Jesus with the Balangao, most of whom could not understand English.)*

9. Why was the Peace Pact important? *(It gave peace a chance and allowed for safe travel between warring tribes. No one would be killed as long as the peace pact held.)*

10. What Bible verses would help you have God's peace in your heart if you were to work as a missionary among warring headhunters? *(Allow students to recite verses aloud, or invite them to search their Bible concordances for the word* peace *and read aloud the verses that are referenced.)*

Chapter 4

1. Why were evil spirits trying to frighten Tekla? *(In searching for God, Tekla had stopped sacrificing to the spirits. They wanted her allegiance forever. They didn't want her to learn the Truth about their God. So they used fear, hoping it would cause her to give up her search for God.)*

2. Why was it very brave for Tekla to break away from her father's beliefs about the spirits and want to know God? *(By being the caretaker of the talking* toeto *spirit, her father was a powerful influence in Tekla's life and with the Balangao. Tekla's desire to turn from the spirits could be misunderstood by her father. She could be thought of as disrespectful.)*

3. How did Tekla help Jo and Anne with the Bible translation work? *(Tekla taught the missionaries many Balangao sounds and words. Then she helped them write the first-ever Balangao alphabet, words and sentences. Eventually, Tekla helped translate the Bible into the Balangao language.)*

4. Explain what Jo meant when she told Tekla she was like the "lost coin" of Luke chapter 15. *(Tekla was separated–lost– from God. Just as the woman in the Bible story treasured the coin and searched desperately for it, so God treasured Tekla. When God sent Jesus to die on the cross, it was God's way of seeking and finding "lost Tekla.")*

5. How was Tekla's life different after she was found by God? *(She could tell God her fears; she experienced God's love, friendship and protection against the spirits; she also could trust Him because He did not lie to her like the spirits.)*

6. What awakened Ama from his sleep one night? *(A dream)*

7. What did the Balangao man in Ama's dream tell him? *(To seriously listen and consider what Jo and Anne had come to Balangao to tell)*

8. What new way of life did God lead Anne to? *(To marry and live with her husband in the USA.)*

9. Why didn't Jo refuse to eat a roasted beetle bug? *(Jo felt it was polite to eat what was offered to her. It was a way of showing Ama and his family that she accepted, not rejected, the Balangao way of life.)*

10. Explain why Canao was glad to see the genealogy of Christ. *(He had only heard tales about the beginning of the world. Now he knew the truth–that there was a Creator God who had the actual names of the world's first people written down in His Book!)*

Chapter 5

1. Complete this sentence: Jo prayed, "Dear Lord, I don't care what you have to do, just teach the Balangao how to really _____!"*(Pray)*

2. Why was Jo concerned that the Balangao learn to pray? *(The Balangao were great problem solvers. It appeared that they could handle their problems very well without God's help. Jo knew that the Bible invited believers to pray and seek God's know-how/wisdom (James 1:5). She wanted the Balangao to see God do the things that they could not do.)*

3. How did God answer Jo's prayer, "just teach the Balangao to pray"? *(He allowed the helicopter crash. That day Jo heard the Balangao pray like never before! They realized God could do what they could not do. "God keep Jo from dying!" they prayed. God answered their prayer. From then on the Balangao learned to "really pray" about everything!)*

4. Finish this Balangao prayer: "God, keep Jo alive so she can _____!" *(Finish the Book. They wanted her to lead the translation team and complete translating the Balangao Bible!)*

5. Tekla was warned by unbelievers, "God will punish you for translating His Word into the Balangao language!" What did Tekla do in spite of these warnings? *(Tekla did not believe the helicopter crash was punishment from God. She kept working together with the translation team until the Balangao Bible translation, was finished.)*

6. If you had been Tekla, how would you have handled the warnings she received? *(Allow your students to answer in their own words.)*

7. What happened to Doming, Canao's son, as a result of the helicopter crash? *(God healed him. He surrendered his life to God and took a year off from college to help Jo with the Balangao Bible translation. He later became a leader in the Balangao church!)*

8. Why do you think Jo honored Canao with the very first printed Balangao New Testament? *(He was a strong, respected Christian leader in the Balangao church who had taken the good news of Jesus to many villages. He was also an excellent "father" to Jo and Anne, and one of the main translation helpers on the Bible translation team.)*

9. Tell me one way you have been "changed by the Book." *(Allow students to give own answers.)*

10. Name something a Christian can do that will "last forever." *(Suggested answers: pray for salvation of friends; read the Bible because the Bible lasts forever (1 Peter 1:25); help my friends to be saved; be a Bible translator!)*